GAME IMPF READING LEVELS

by

Jim McNicholas

and

Joe McEntee

A NASEN Publication

Published by NASEN.
NASEN is a registered charity. Charity No. 1007023.
NASEN is a company limited by guarantee, registered in England and Wales. Company No. 2674379.

Further copies of this book and details of NASEN's many other publications may be obtained from the Publications Department at its registered office: NASEN House, 4/5, Amber Business Village, Amber Close, Amington, Tamworth, Staffs. B77 4RP.
Tel: 01827 311500; Fax: 01827 313005
Email: welcome@nasen.org.uk

Printed in the United Kingdom by Stowes, Stoke-on-Trent.

CONTENTS

INTRODUCTION

Why Games?
The advantages of using games
Some cautionary points

A COMPENDIUM OF GAMES LISTED BY PRE-READING AND READING SKILLS

WORD ATTACK SKILLS/WORD BUILDING

READING FOR MEANING

PAPER AND PENCIL GAMES TO IMPROVE READING AND WRITING

USING GAMES TO DEVELOP THE SIGHT VOCABULARY OF A READING SCHEME

USING GAMES TO DEVELOP PHONIC SKILLS

INTRODUCTION

Any new edition of a book on reading games would be incomplete without reference to National Curriculum requirements. What this book attempts to do, therefore, is to suggest games and activities which can help children to achieve attainment at their appropriate reading level. For example, a considerable number of games are devoted to Attainment Target 2 : Reading, Level 1 (b) 'begin to recognise individual words or letters in familiar contexts', and to Level 2 (c) 'use picture and context cues, words recognised on sight and phonic cues in reading' (see *English in the National Curriculum*, DES and Welsh Office, 1989).

However, there is no deliberate intention to relate games and activities directly to Key Stages, Levels, or Statements of Attainment. For example, it just happens that Game 60 contributes to Level 3 (e) 'bring to their writing and discussion about stories some understanding of the way stories are structured'. The aim is to put the case for using a games approach and, by showing how many of them have been adapted from traditional sources, encourage further adaptation and improvisation. Ideally, parents and teachers will use these games and their own inventiveness to create appropriate learning activities which match the individual learners needs at the required level.

It is important to recognise that the programme of study designed with individual children in mind remains the starting point for the learning activity. The games and activities herein are to be viewed as vehicles for helping to stimulate development in the structuring of language and reading ability within the overall programme of study.

It must be stressed that games are not being advocated as a means of teaching reading in isolation. The recent 1990s debate on teaching methods, like similar methodological issues over the past four decades, seems to have been interpreted by the protagonists as vindication for their own polarized viewpoints. A more common-sense view would suggest an eclectic approach. HMI, for instance, endorse a 'mix of methods' (*The Teaching and Learning of Reading in Primary Schools*, DES, 1990 para 76).

Many children, immersed in the world where appropriate language is used and encouraged, in which interesting stories are read to them, and where exciting pictures and books surround them, may learn to read smoothly using a 'real books' approach. Other pupils, perhaps from impoverished environmental backgrounds or for reasons which may indicate sensory or speech difficulties or other specific factors, will need a heavily structured approach to developing the skills of reading. Whatever the methods used, a systematic programme in which pupils' progress may be monitored, discussed and guided, is essential.

1

Within the programme, there may well be a place for phonics, vocabulary building, or help in the use of context and reading for meaning. Language experience and story methods may be preferred. This should not lead to pupils completing pages of exercises or, for that matter, playing reading games in isolation from reading books or real-life language. There is no evidence to suggest that there is a transfer of knowledge from isolated exercises into a generalised framework of skills. So, for example, the teaching of phonics should arise from a natural instance in reading and should be incidence-specific.

Within this context, it is suggested that the games and activites described in the following pages should be used selectively in a planned way within the framework of the well-organised programme. The games and activities have been gathered into various categories of reading skills : left to right orientation, initial letter sounds, sight vocabulary, word attack skills, reading for meaning, etc. Again, it is not intended to promote teaching reading by isolated skills. The categorisation and collation is provided to help where perhaps an analysis of need shows that some specific teaching input is required. Such skills overlap and smoothness and fluency will always be a factor in selecting any particular activity. However, an ongoing assessment of level of performance and the child's own preferences, may indicate a need for games to build confidence, provide repetition, and to ensure both success and enjoyment.

WHY GAMES?

From earliest infancy there appears to be in children an instinctive interest for play. Young children learn most of their concepts of self, constancy, orientation, size and number by playing games. Those pre-school children fortunate to have had adults to play with them I-Spy. 'Kim's Game', rhyming games and to re-tell nursery rhymes usually commence school with a well developed facility for language.

At school, some children spend most of their free time in playing games. Many teachers have recognised the quite tremendous powers of energy, enthusiasm and motivation that lie within these instincts and interests. Could not a games approach to learning be used in and outside the classroom to provide a stimulus and to sustain interest for learning in all children?

Television and the sophisticated toys of today have robbed children of the imaginative play enjoyed by former generations. They come to school unaware, in many cases, of initial sounds (previously learned in street games), not knowing rhymes (once learned in skipping games), ignorant of concepts 'up' 'down', 'under', and so forth (which they surely would have absorbed in games of 'Follow the leader' and 'Simon Says').

The teacher's task is to analyse each child's needs and then to frame a programme to suit them. Questions one would ask in such an analysis might include the following:–

Does this child need – a games approach at this stage of learning?

                – motivating?

                – games to develop concentration?

                – games to provide pleasurable learning?

Sometimes a child who has been deprived of games can be seen at school voluntarily playing a game which a much younger child would call 'babyish'. It seems as if there is a need for a child not to lose any of the stages of growing-up, provided in part by playing games. Whether this is a correct hypothesis or not, it appears that children derive a certain amount of emotional release from playing games. In the case of a very young child whose early attempts at reading have resulted in complete failure, a strong dislike of books may develop. Such a child may virtually refuse to look at a reading book. In such an instance, games must be designed to overcome that particular problem. In other words, the selection of games chosen to be used must result in that child being able to pick up a reading book, no matter how simple, and to be able to read it. One effective way of achieving this is to devise games which use the vocabulary of that

3

particular book. These games must be played until there is no possibility of the child failing. Once that first book has been conquered, very often the fear of reading and the dislike of reading books will vanish, and the child will probably continue to make progress. Games can be a source of learning at a subliminal level and, as this learning is achieved in a pleasurable way, progress can be made both academically and emotionally.

THE ADVANTAGES OF USING GAMES

1. Children will respond usually without inhibitions and are readily observed at their most natural.
2. The child's level of ability is more easily determinable.
3. Games allow class and teacher to share in some fun and to develop good relationships.
4. Lessons can be varied, and reading can be a source of fun and excitement – something to look forward to.
5. Emotionally, good games can release tensions, help work off surplus energy and frustrations.
6. Children can achieve feelings of success and grow in confidence.
7. Motivation to learn is stimulated.
8. Repetition can be provided whilst avoiding the chore of repeating previous effort.
9. Games help to encourage the development of social skills such as working together, sharing and taking turns.
10. In the process of playing reading games, many aspects of speaking and listening, outlined in Attainment Target 1 of National Curriculum English, will have been achieved quite naturally. For example, Level 1,a 'participate as speakers and listeners in group activities'; Level 2,a 'participate as speakers and listeners in a group engaged in a given task'; Level 1,c/2,e – responding appropriately to simple/complex instructions.

SOME CAUTIONARY POINTS

1. Games must not replace a well-structured reading programme; rather, they fit into such a scheme and supplement it where required.
2. Teachers should watch for signs of obsolescence and reject games when over-learning is reached and before boredom sets in.
3. There should be a check on games to ensure that learning is in fact taking place.

4. There is a danger of playing games for games' sake. Remember – they should be used to develop specific aspects of reading.

5. Teachers and children should understand the purpose of the game. The limitations in 'Word Lotto' for example, the child can only respond correctly if he or she already knows what a 'called' word says.

   Some games encourage success without the use of reading skill. For example, Lotto games in which words are written below pictures; also a symbol game in which a child pieces cards together thus:–

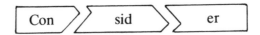

Con ⟩ sid ⟩⟩ er

In the latter activity, a child could succeed by correctly putting together the card shapes.

6. Do not assume that the child will learn what the teacher intended to teach. In an exercise to develop sentence comprehension a child has been given a picture of a ship with the words 'The ship sails away' written below it. The child has these words on individual cards and has to place the four words in the correct sentence order. But does it improve sentence comprehension? Does it merely require a visual match?

7. In an exercise of aural discrimination to select the stranger from 'rat', 'pat', 'hat', 'sit', 'fat' – do not let the child work alone from a written exercise. Do not assume that s/he will sound out each word, it is quite possible s/he will use visual discrimination to find the answer. Aural discrimination requires: *sound – listening – response – assessment*.

8. Commercial games such as *Lexicon*, *Scrabble* and *Spill and Spell* have some motivation value but only provide practice in known words. As the games proceed, the words that can be composed are restricted by the letters available.

9. In schools, it would seem prudent to avoid making games too fiercely competitive. Some children may react adversely when they cannot succeed or when one or two competitors outshine them easily. Competition may stimulate some children to try harder; in others, particularly the emotionally disturbed, it may only increase partisanship and aggression.

10. Teachers need to ask:–
    - what does the child need?
    - will this activity fulfil that need?
    - how will I assess that learning has taken place?
    - what is the next step in the learning process?

A COMPENDIUM OF GAMES

The games described below are of a kind that can be made using the simplest and least expensive of materials. Most of the activities will be recognised by many readers as adaptations of childhood favourites from street, playground, Cub or Brownie meetings and other such origins that provide motivating vehicles for learning in schools.

1. **To Develop Body Image**   All Change

   Children in pairs. Teacher calls out 'Shoulder to Shoulder' – children stand shoulder to shoulder; toe to toe, etc. On call 'All Change' children find new partners.

2. **Spatial Concepts**   Simon Says

   Simon says 'Jump on the wall', etc. It might be found necessary to have the concepts illustrated by drawings. Younger children could make a cat and mouse with plasticine and so instructions 'Chase mouse around a box – mouse hides under the box – cat jumps over etc.'

3. **Left/Right Discrimination**   Follow-the-Leader

   Follow a command 'Right hand on right shoulder'. 'Left hand on right ear', etc.

4. **Left-to-Right**   Moving Right

   (a)   Children sit in chairs arranged in rows. 'Change left' is called. Child on left runs to extreme right as others have all moved left. 'Change right' is called and child on right moves to extreme left. (Played at speed as fast as children can cope.)

   (b)   'Run to touch wall nearest to your left side – your right side'. 'Point right. Point left. Swing right leg to right. Left leg to left'.

5. **Left-Right Body Awareness**   Left/Right Tick

A large or small group activity.

One child is appointed 'man' or 'woman' – s/he has to catch someone and place the piece of adhesive paper (red for left hand, arm, leg or foot – blue for the right hand, arm, leg or foot) on the appropriate left or right side of the person caught. The person caught is 'man' or 'woman' *unless* the adhesive paper has been stuck on wrong side, i.e. blue paper was placed on his/her left leg.

Teachers should look out for child whose left-right awareness is weak, and give him/her special attention.

6. **To Help Auditory Discrimination**   Musical Chairs

Children sit when music stops, but there is one less seat than there are children, so the last one is out each time it stops. Use other sounds instead of music. Teacher can recite word families and insert a 'wrong' word: 'ball', 'hall', 'fall', 'well', 'tall' – when 'well' is called children should sit. This is a particularly difficult one to hear but it illustrates the point.

A word of advice – if playing the game with many children, split them into smaller groups, and keep the ones with the weakest auditory skills in one group.

7. **Auditory Discrimination**   Match the Sound

Children skip in a ring until the command 'Stop'. Teacher throws ball or bag to child and says a word. Before 10 is counted, child calls another word with same sound (beginning, ending, vowel, blend etc.)

8. **Auditory Recall** Remember the Word

Class or group activity.

Teacher calls out five words then displays four of the words. Children are asked to name the missing word. One point for each correct response – child with most points is the winner.

9. **Teaching Initial Letter**   Man or Woman from Space

One child is 'man'. Children call out 'Man from Space may I chase?' He replies 'Yes if your name begins like duck' (or fox, etc.). Children with this initial chase him. The one who catches him is the new 'man'. The same procedure is used if the child concerned is a Woman from Space.

10. **Initial Letters or Vocabulary Building**   Soldier on the Bridge

Variation of 9. Children call out 'Soldier on the Bridge may we pass?' Soldier says 'Yes, if your name begins with . . ., or if you have a colour g . . .' (b . . ., etc.). S/he tries to catch them.

Can be used to increase vocabulary. Give each child name of an animal. Soldier on Bridge allows to pass 'If you can bark. If you can roar, etc'.

11. **Letter/Word Recognition**   Find the Square

Letters are written in chalk on playground flags or drawn squares. Teacher calls out a letter. First child to jump in the square is the winner.

For letters substitute words that need reinforcement: likewise opposites, rhymes, words that end the same, have the same vowel sound.

12. **Letter Recognition**   Cats and Mice

When word beginning with C is called, mice chase cats.
When word beginning with M is called, cats chase mice.

Team scores when it touches goal without being tagged.

Alternatives (a) Use any letters.
               (b) One team vowels, one team consonants.
               (c) Words that end with . . .

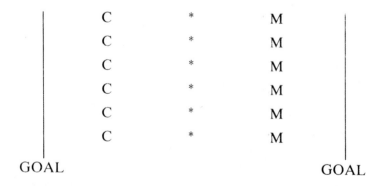

13. **Teaching Vowel Sounds**   Steal the Beans

Children are divided into teams of, say, five-lettered thus:

Team A		Team B
a		u
e	Beans	o
i	(bean bag)	i
o		e
u		a

Teacher calls out a word. If the word begins with one of these letters, the children whose letter it is rush to the bean bag and try to get it back before being tagged.

In addition to the auditory skills, visual recognition can be heightened by giving children words on a card. For example, teacher shows the word 'apple'. The two children labelled 'a' rush to the beans.

14. **Teaching Capital and Small Letters**   Turn and Chase

Two teams face the same direction. Team 1 has, say, capitals; team 2 small letters. On signal from teacher, one child in team 1 finds corresponding child in team 2, touches him or her and runs around the team to his/her place before being caught by child from team 2.

Example – D is touched by teacher. S/he touches 'd' and runs in direction shown. D is dotted line, 'd' is continuous.

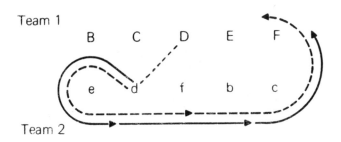

15. **Letter Sounds**   I Spy Pictures

A very useful activity to engage large or small groups, or a whole class.

Pin 26 small envelopes around the room and letter A – Z.
Have the children copy pictures and words from picture
dictionaries on cards small enough to slip into the envelopes.
When there are a number of cards in each envelope, the game can
be played. Teacher asks a child to take a card from, say the 'f'
envelope. The child walks to envelope, selects a card and is careful
not to show it to anyone. Then by giving a verbal clue or mime
invites the group to guess what is on the card.
The winner selects the next card.

16. **Letter Sounds**   Guess the Picture

Pictures are pasted on to small cards. On the other side is written
the initial letter sound.

The pack is placed picture-side up on a table. Children take a
card in turn and say the sound that the picture 'begins with' – then
the card is turned over and the child looks at the letter – if s/he was
correct s/he keeps the card; if not the card goes to the bottom of
the pack.

Note: allow the child to decide, on looking at the letter, if s/he is
correct or not.

Teacher should note which letters give difficulty and prepare
more activities to help overcome them.

17. **Letter Recognition**   Guess the Letter

Use of the tactile sense.

Recommended highly for children who do not catch on quickly to
recall letters: especially useful for cases of letter-reversal and
confusion.

Letters made of wood, cardboard or plastic are placed in the
hands of a child. With his/her eyes shut – and his/her hands in
front – s/he must say the name of the letter. If correct, s/he keeps
the letter.

When a child gets many incorrect answers, s/he should be given
further letter work – making letters in a sand tray; making letters
of plasticine, tracing letters. Later, the child can return to 'Guess
the Letter' and other letter recognition games.

18. **Visual Discrimination**   Word Shapes,

(a)   Class activity.

Ten words are taken from children's reader. The words are written on one blackboard. Their shapes are drawn on another. Class is asked to compare words and shapes and see how they fit. (Shapes could be drawn around some words.)

Class is asked to write down words and put correct shapes around them.

(b)   Group activity.

Words taken from reader. Children work in pairs. Each child has a sheet of paper on which shapes of words are drawn; s/he has the words on card and these have been cut to the same shape. Children take it in turns to match shapes by placing card on the sheet and saying the word. Each tries to get his or her sheet full.

e.g.

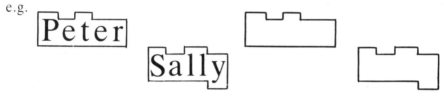

19. **Visual Discrimination**   Half Words

Children work in pairs.

Take words that children are encountering in their class readers or from language experience and make a list for display. A pencil line can be drawn horizontally through the middle of each word. Copy each half word on card. Children see how quickly they can match up words and say them.

A further activity would be to see how quickly children recognise a word from seeing half of the configuration only. This could be a class activity. Note that the top half of the word gives us most clue recognition.

20. **Visual Word Recall**   Memory Game

Group game.

Place five words on the table, get children to cover their eyes and remove one card – then ask them to name the missing word. The game can be made more difficult by increasing the number of words and by removing more than one card.

This can be a class activity if written on the blackboard.

21. **To Build Sight Vocabulary**   Hop Scotch

Played in playground or hall. A word recognition game. As the children hop into a square the word written in the square is called out.

In addition to reading, left – right training can be incorporated. Children can be told to start in top left hand corner, to go from left to right 'just as words are written in books'. The challenge of the game is to hop as far as possible from start without standing on any lines and, of course, saying as many words as possible. Two teams could compete by having two courses side by side.

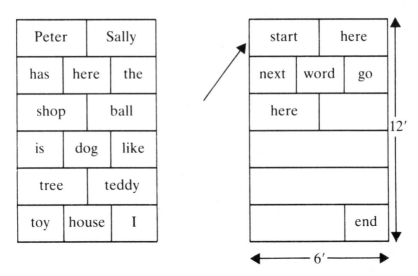

Alternative to children individually calling out the words, the whole class could call as child reaches a word. After playing a few times it will be obvious which words are well-known; these can be replaced by newer words.

For children with a good physical co-ordination, a stone or bean-bag could be kicked into the next square before hopping into it.

22. **A Word Recognition Game**   Squirrel Chase

Children in circle with hands behind the back. The 'squirrel' shows children a card with a word on it. Then s/he walks round the circle and puts the card in one child's hand. On calling out the word s/he chases the squirrel round the outside of the circle. The child who does not catch the squirrel, becomes the new squirrel.

23. **Word Recognition** Word Hop

Teacher holds up flash card. Calls on one child to say word. If correct, child takes one hop to teacher.

24. **Vocabulary Building** Duster Relay

Children in two teams. Lists of words are written on blackboard. Child comes out with duster and says a word it can recognise and then erases it and runs back to next child with duster. This game and 45 can be used for synonyms, homonyms, etc.

25. **Word Recognition** Mark the Word

Two identical lists of words are written on blackboard – one list for each team but in different order. When teacher calls out a word number 1 pair run out and draw a line under the word. Then number 2 pair and so on. Winner is recorded; team with most points wins.

26. **Sight Vocabulary Building** Football 1

Two teams. Blackboard made out as a football pitch on which is drawn lines. As a child gets a word correct a ball is drawn on the next line towards opponent's goal.

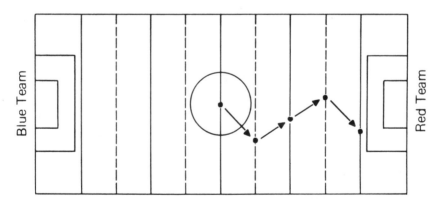

Example – Blue team kicks off. One child in team reads first word 'face'. Red team's turn. Word is 'race'. Child called on says 'rack'. (Opportunity to show the difference.) Gets it wrong so ball goes further to Red's goal. Blue team get this word right so ball goes further to Red goal. The Blue's turn. 'Space' read correctly – ball goes on line nearest Red's goal. Reds have to read next word correctly to save a goal.

27. **Sight Vocabulary Building** Snakes and Ladders

Played as ordinary Snakes and Ladders. Penalty squares e.g. 'Go back to No. 4'; reward squares e.g. 'Have another turn'. A child is not penalised for not knowing a word except in the case of a star word which carries either a penalty or a reward. If a child gets a star word correct s/he has another turn, if not, s/he goes back to the number written by the star. (See illustration.)

Game 27.   SNAKES AND LADDERS

Long e̅ sound

24 heel	* **15** 25 queen	26 leap	27 Back to 22	28 she	29 read
23 Have another turn.	22 seat	21 meat	* **12** 20 team	19 fear	
13 Back to 7	* **7** 14 seem	15 tree	16 deep	* **10** 17 dear	18 feed
12 be	11 seed	10 seal	9 real	8 Have another turn.	7 meet
1 bee	2 fee	3 Have another turn.	4 heat	* **2** 5 jeep	6 Back to one.

28. **Sight Vocabulary Building**   Pairs in Concentration

Each word is on two cards. Cards spread out and face down. Child turns over two cards and tries to find matching pair. If child fails to get a pair s/he replaces them in the same place face down. When a pair is found child has another turn. Winner is the child with most cards when the table is cleared.

29. **Word Recognition**   Grab

Same flash cards as for 28. This time cards are placed with words uppermost. Child grabs when teacher calls a word. Penalty – should child grab wrong card s/he must replace all the ones that s/he has collected previously. This is a very useful game to develop both aural and visual discrimination. If one of the words is 'flag' teacher can call out 'flap' and the children will easily mistake the words if not careful.

30. **Word Recognition**   Find the Word

Each child has a list of words. The words are also on cards face down. Child picks up card, reads it and if that word is on his or her list, s/he places the card over the word. If not, he or she replaces it. The other children check their lists and if the word is on their list they must try to remember where the card is placed so they can pick it up when their turn comes around.

**In the next four games the flash cards are used in place of dice.
The backs of the cards are numbered 1 – 6.**

31. **Sight Vocabulary Building**   Football 2

    For two children or two small teams.

    Large card ruled at one inch intervals on drawing of a football
    pitch. Use a counter for ball. Child reads flash card. If correct s/he
    moves counter forward the number of spaces indicated by the
    number on the back of the flash card; if s/he fails to read the word,
    s/he goes back by the same number.
    Object to score goals.

    Variation – 'Shoot In' – which the teacher can use with just one
    child. Start the counter at the halfway line and s/he moves forward
    towards goal as above.

32. **Sight Vocabulary Building**   Ladder Game

    Played exactly the same way as football. Takes very short time as
    there are no penalties. For each word correct, team moves its
    counter higher up the ladder. Winner – first team to reach the top.

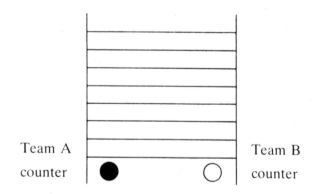

33. **Sight Vocabulary**   Racetrack

Played on a track or card or blackboard with counters or 'horses' etc. Again played in exactly the same way. Can be horse racing, motor cycling or car racing. Various penalties to ensure repetition of words, e.g. 'Bad skid go back six places'.

34. **Sight Vocabulary**   Ludo

Ordinary Ludo card and counters. Played in ordinary way using flash cards as dice. No penalties as game takes considerable time.

35. **Word Recognition**   Tiddlywinks

Words written in shapes. Each shape carries a score.
Counters are flicked on to shapes. Child scores if s/he reads the word. Alternatively, the shapes can be numbered corresponding to a list on blackboard or wall. Child gets No. 6 – reads the word at No. 6 on list.

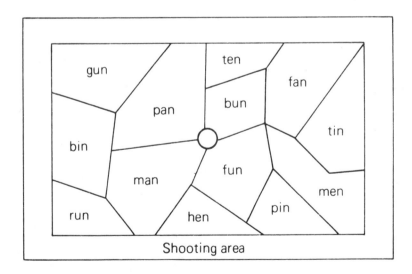

Shooting area

36. **Sight Vocabulary**   Route to Goal

Four packs of cards. Each pack in a separate colour.
The arrows and rectangles are similarly coloured. On some of the
cards are stars. First player takes a card and places it in first
square. If s/he says it correctly, s/he picks up next card and puts it
in the next square indicated by arrow. If wrong, opponent says the
word, or if it is a star word, opponent 'tackles', that is, says the
word and proceeds on same pack towards goal.

When a goal is scored start on any other pack. If neither team
can say a word, it is a 'bounce-up'. Referee (teacher or another
child) helps with the word. The first one to call the word takes
over the route to goal.

ROUTE TO GOAL

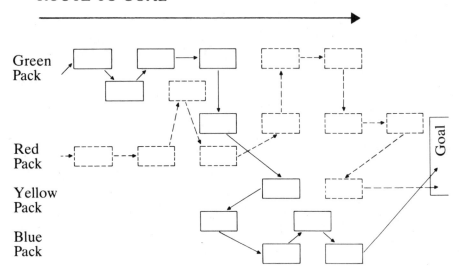

37. **Word Recognition**   Quickie

Group game – preferably played after Grab (29) or other such games.

(a)   Teacher has pack of cards to be read. He or she turns over a card in front of one child and immediately places his or her hand over it. If the child calls it, he or she receives the card, if not the next child has that turn and, if correct, his or her own word. Children must look at all the words turned over and really concentrate. Teacher can vary speed of the operation according to ability of the pupils. The quicker pupils see the word only for an instant and some form of subliminal recognition takes place. Winner, of course, is the one with the most cards.

(b)   To prevent 'word barking' – especially for children who point to words and read slowly one word at a time, make phrases on card 'I see Jane', 'Here is Peter', 'Here they are' and play 'Quickie'.

38. **Word Recognition**   Charlie Chaplin

Could be used as a spelling exercise.

Children work in pairs. Teacher gives each child a list of words taken from the class reader. First child puts on paper a number of dashes – a dash for each letter of a word s/he selects from his or her list. Second player has to guess the word. S/he says a letter and if it is in the word, first child inserts that letter, e.g. S/he calls out 'e' – No. 1 inserts 'e'.

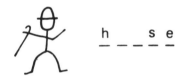

Then s/he says 'a'. This is not in the word so No. 1 draws a hat.
No. 2 says 'r'. Not in the word so No. 1 draws a head.
No. 2 says 'b'. Not in the word so No. 1 draws a body.
No. 2 says 'h'. No. 1 inserts it.
No. 2 says 's'. No. 1 inserts it.
No. 2 says 'horse' – Wrong so No. 1 draws a leg.
No. 2 says 'house' – Correct.
– Other player's turn.

Game continues till Charlie Chaplin is drawn. Loser is 'Charlie Chaplin'.

19

39. **Sight Vocabulary Building**   Cricket

(See illustration)

A game for two teams of up to four on each side. Of interest particularly to older children.

Batting

First team rolls die and takes a card from the pack corresponding to the number of the die. For example, if the die shows 4, the player takes a card from the pack numbered 4, if the player can read the word, s/he scores 4 runs for his or her team; If s/he cannot, the 'umpire' tells him or her the word and the card goes to the bottom of the pack and a score is not given. The die is handed to the next player in the team and so on. In each pack are interspersed words: – 'caught', 'run out', 'bowled', 'stumped'. When these are turned over, the whole team is out. Then the other team bats. It is possible for teams to have several innings in the course of one game.

Game 39.   CRICKET

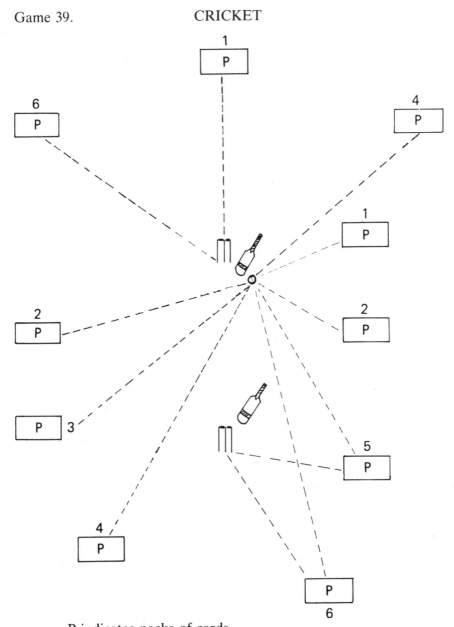

P indicates packs of cards.
E.g. child throws die – gets 5. Takes from 5 pack.

40. **Sight Vocabulary**   Target

(See illustration.)

A game for up to six players.

Each player takes a turn to flick or throw a counter on to the target. Players take a card from the pack according to the number landed on. If card is read successfully, player gets that number of points.

Score only if player can say the word on the card; if unable to say the word, other players say it. All words are replaced at the bottom of the pack.

This game is especially suitable for younger and more restive children. The activity of throwing/flicking and reading help them to work off their restlessness and develop co-ordination.

TARGET

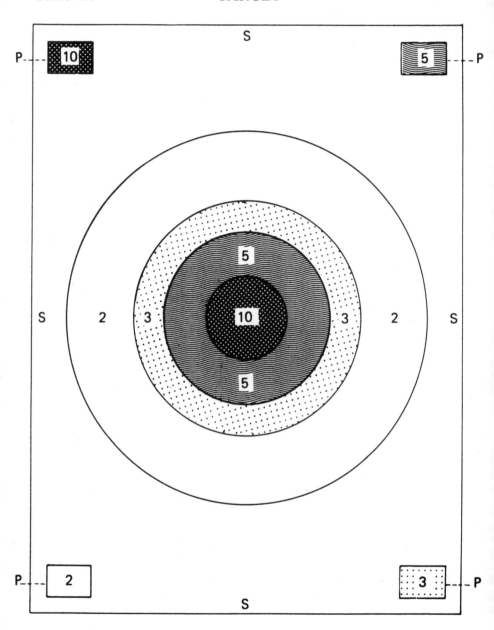

P indicates packs of cards. Scores according to the number of the pack.
S indicates shooting area.

41. **Sight Vocabulary**   Soccer

(See illustration.)

Older boys, particularly, like this game.

Game for two to eight players – two teams, one red, one blue.
In the diagram, the black rings are blue players, the 'x' rings are red
players. Proceeding from each ring are three arrows numbered 1 – 2,
3 – 4, 5 – 6. Toss a coin for kick-off.
Team winning the toss take the (counter) ball at the centre circle.
A pack of cards with words and numbers 1 – 6 on them provide the
basis for movement on the field of play. On reading a card
successfully, the player notes the number on the card and moves the
counter in the direction of the arrow so numbered.

Note that an arrow from each player goes to an opponent, so that
play is fast-flowing and all over the field. Near the goal the 'forwards'
shooting at goal may score or miss.

When word is not known, the opposing team may say the word.
If successful, they obtain possession. If neither team knows the word,
the referee helps with the word and the first team to call the word gains
possession.

Once six words have been learned, one or two news ones can be
substituted until all six are new, and gradually with much over-learning
the players' sight vocabulary is enlarged.

Game 41. SOCCER

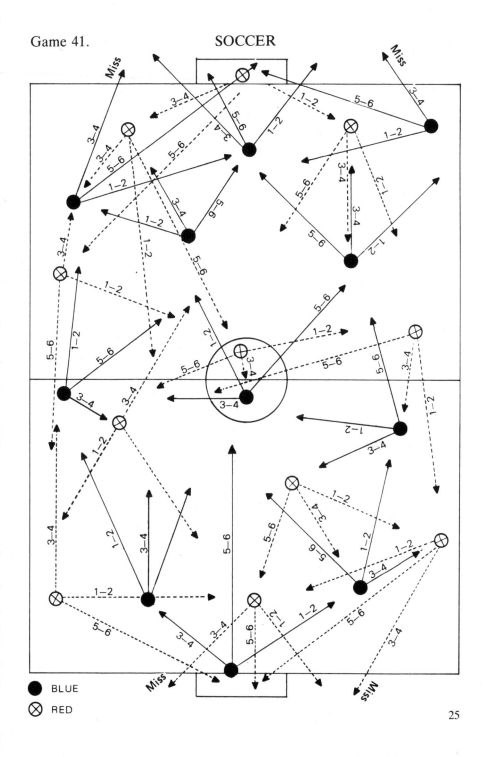

BLUE ●

RED ⊗

25

42. **Blends**   Change the Circle

(Could be used to teach other skills.)

Each child is given a card with a word blend. Several children have the same blend. When a word is called with this blend, they hold them up and change places. One child from centre of circle tries to get into an empty space.

Example – Teacher calls out 'sting'. Three children have cards with digraph 'st' written on them. They hold up the card and attempt to change places by running around the circle. In the drawing No. 1 runs to 6. Number 6 runs to 4. Number 4 runs to space at No. 1. Before No. 4 gets there the Man or Woman in the Middle runs into the space, so No. 4 is now 'man or woman'.

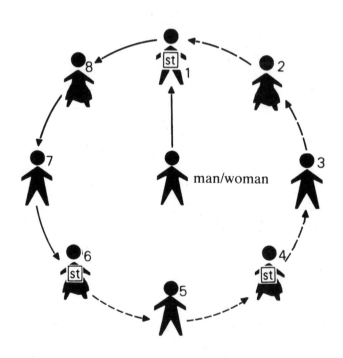

43. **Blends**   Mouse and Cheese

Children run round circle and through original gap to the 'cheese' (bean bag). Instead of calling out the sound the teacher can hold up a card with digraph, e.g. 'ch', 'sh', or a word containing the digraph.

Example: two children have 'ch' sound. They run round as indicated – one the dotted circle, the other a continuous circle, to see who gets the bean bag first.

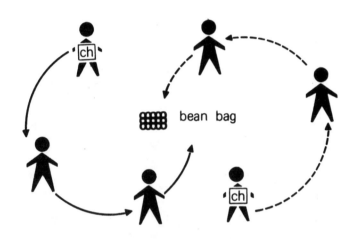

bean bag

44. **Word Building**   Change a Letter

Children in circle. The teacher calls out a word and tosses bean bag to a child. Child gives a different word changing one letter, and tosses bean bag into basket (one point given for each success). E.g. Teacher calls out 'bat', child calls out 'hat' or 'bet' or 'bad'.

45. **Rhymes/Word Building**   Blackboard Relay

Children in teams. Team A is given a word, say, 'bat'; team B 'net'. On the word 'go', first child in each team runs to blackboard and writes a word that rhymes with the first word. Then s/he runs and gives the chalk to second child and so on. Teacher helps children having difficulty. First team to finish wins.

46. **Blends**   Word Draughts

A game for two players. (See illustration.)

Each player has four draughts.

Black starts and travels only on black squares, white on white.
As a square is reached the player calls out the word; if not known
s/he is told the word but goes back one place, then it is white's
turn, and so on. Winner is first to get all four draughts home.
The game can be played on draughts board.
Chinagraph pencils rub off easily on the glossy board.
(If the board has lost its gloss cover first with cellophane.)

Alternatively, use small blackboards and chalk or make out
boards on paper 8″ x 8″.

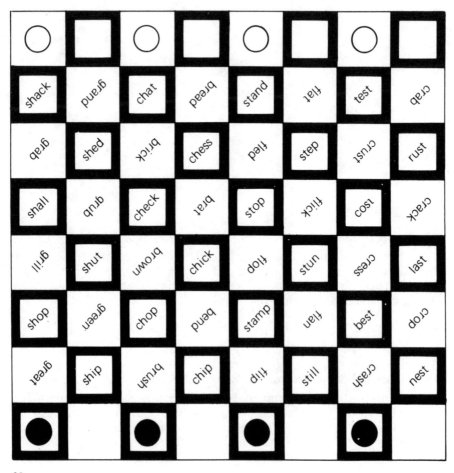

47. **Word Building**   Word Oxo

(See illustration.)

Played by two players on paper. One has a red pencil, the other a blue pencil.

A square is drawn in which the initial letters of three letter words are given. Players take turns to add a letter. If the letter completes a word, the player adding that letter crosses the word out and adds a letter to another word. If a player cannot go the other player takes his or her turn.

b	e	t	e	a	p	d	o	g
f	o	x	g			h		
j		k				l		
m		n				p		
r		s				t		
v		w				y		
b		d				s		
h		r				m		
n		p				b		

For instance in game illustrated to teach vowels, all words are of three letters. The next letter to be added must be a vowel.

Player 1. Red (dotted line for our purposes).

Player 2. Blue (continuous line).

Red puts 'e'. Blue adds 't' and makes the word bat. Blue draws a blue line through bat and puts 'a' after 'c'. Red adds 'p' to make 'cap', draws a red line through 'cap' and puts 'o' after 'd'. Blue cannot complete the word so Red adds 'g' to make 'dog'. S/he then has another turn and adds 'o' to 'f' which Blue converts to 'fox'. Score at this stage 2 – 2. Winner is the one with most lines/ words to his or her credit.

To make words of four letter length use a square 8″ x 8″.

If wanting to use final 'e' use formation thus:-

h	o	m	e	d	u	k	e
	a		e		i		e
	o		e		a		e
	u		e		a		e
c	h			c	h		
c	h			c	h		
		c	h			c	h
		c	h			c	h

First player, Red, puts in first consonant of word 'h'.
Second player, Blue, adds another consonant 'm'. Then Blue puts 'd' and Red adds 'k' to make duke. Score 1 – 1.

If teaching 'ch' – put in 'ch' as shown. Play as the other game.

48. **To Foster Phonic Discrimination**   Check It

An adaptation of Stott's Porthole* activity, played by two children.

One child has a card with 20 pictures, each numbered and a word under each picture.

The other child has a card with the same 20 words (no pictures) but in a different order. Beside each word is drawn a one inch square with a smaller square cut out inside it:-

Under this card is an answer sheet attached to card by clips, with 20 one-inch squares in the same position as the squares on the cardboard. In the corners of these squares are numbers which give the answers.

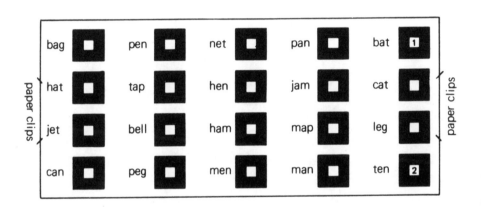

Child A calls out the words thus: 'Number one – bat'.

Child B has to find the word 'bat' on his or her card and write '1' in the square by 'bat'.

Child A – 'Number two – ten'.

Child B finds this – last word, bottom line and writes '2' in this square.

When 20 have been completed the answer sheet is detached and both children check the results with the numbers on the corner of each square on the answer sheet.

* Taken from the Stott *Programmed Reading Kit* published by Holmes McDougall. Now out-of-print.

A well-constructed activity can ensure that the children discriminate and sound each letter in a word. The game can be used as a diagnostic test and the record is provided on the answer sheet.

In the example provided, the child has to make distinction between vowels 'a' and 'e', and in some cases between final consonants. This activity could be given to children who know letter sounds but need practice at blending, and to children who guess from initial letters or who fail to read the middle of a word.

Obviously this activity lends itself to help in both the testing and practice of letter sounds and initial and final consonantal blends. Improvisations could well lead to further adaptation.

49. **Word Building**   Word Wheel

A class activity.

Instead of individual word wheels, a large class wheel could be made. Most word wheels seen have too many blends and digraphs. Make it simple – use as in diagram – new sounds to be learned can be slotted in with Sellotape. Prepare children adequately by pointing out the digraph sound 'ou' and often.

To play: two teams – teacher spins the wheel and asks one child to say the word formed. If it makes a proper word s/he must say 'yes' to obtain a point for his or her team. Then this child spins the wheel and asks a child from the other team to say the word formed. If this player does not know the word, s/he must say it or forfeit a point.

For further use: children could write down each word as it is formed by the 'wheel', thereby reinforcing learning by making each child concentrate on the word, its sound and written form.

Game 1

Words: 'round', 'pound', 'mound', 'hound', 'sound', 'found'.

Game 2

Taped digraph 'ai'.   Fixed wheel at letter 'l'.
Words: pail, mail, hail, sail, fail, rail.

Game 49.   WORD WHEEL

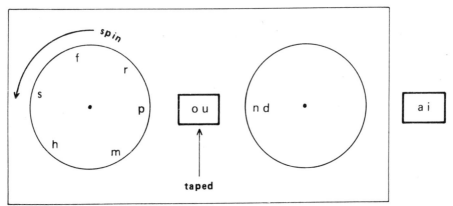

50. **Teaching Syllabication**   The Syllable Game

For two players or two small teams.

Words of two syllables are written on card. The first syllable on blue card, the second on red, The blue cards are dealt and the children take it in turn to pick up a red card and see if they blend to make a word. Extend to three syllable words using yellow card for third syllable.

Alternatively, lay out blue cards then deal red cards and ask children to place red cards in position to make words. Also use for compound words.

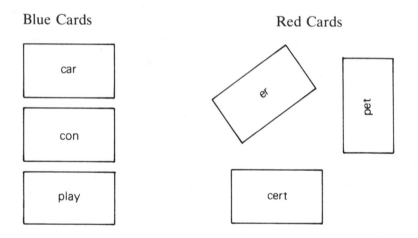

51. **Phonic Discrimination** Pictographs

A class activity.

(a) The alphabet is written down and each letter illustrated by an object which has that letter's initial sound and, as far as possible, contains the letter shape. (See illustration.)

Words in the form of pictographs are drawn on cards and the children are challenged to de-code the pictures.

Examples:-

FAT

SUN

Many exercises can be devised with illustrations drawn on the blackboard. Children can challenge each other in small groups to de-code their codes.

N.B. Start with three letter words, then four, etc.

(b) Word-Building. Making pictographs.

Teacher calls out words slowly, and children make the pictographs.

These exercises have been found useful with children who have auditory-visual weakness. The drawings help, for instance, to pin-point the difference between 'a' and 'e'. Blends can be easily demonstrated too.

Aa Jj Ss
Bb Kk Tt
Cc Ll Uu
Dd Mm Vv
Ee Nn Ww
Ff Oo Yy
Gg Pp Zz
Hh Qq
Ii Rr

52. **Blends**   Battleships

(See illustration)

A game for up to four players-a-side, and could be adapted to class use. Use for teaching blends and other phonograms.

Each team has a chart marked off in seven rows and seven columns; the rows are numbered 1 – 7, the columns are lettered A – G.

There are seven words in each row and the words on each chart are the same in each row but in a different order. Each team has seven cards on which a ship is drawn, and these are placed on each row at the team's discretion.

Teams take turns to call out the number of the row and a word – if a ship is covering that word the ship is sunk. Winner is the team with the most ships left at the end of the game.
Players have to match word called with the words on the row and say 'no' if it is not a 'hit'. Players get help from each other.

Alternatively, the number and letter of columns can be called out and the team has to announce the word. If a ship is on that word, it is sunk.

BATTLESHIPS

Team One's Card

	A	B	C	D	E	F	G
1	shop	ship	shed	shut	shell		shock
2	shot		shun	shall	shops	ships	sheds
3	rush	rash	mash		mesh	dish	dash
4		wish	fish	gosh	posh	lash	sash
5	chop	chip		chat	chick	chin	chess
6	chill	chug	chap	check	much	such	
7	match	fetch	catch	ditch		latch	patch

Team Two's Card

	A	B	C	D	E	F	G
1	shed	shut		shack	shock	shell	ship
2		shin	shot	sheds	ships	shall	shops
3	mesh	rush	rash	mush	mash	dash	
4	gosh	posh	gash		lash	sash	fish
5	chip		chin	chick	chat	chop	chum
6	chap	check	chug	rich		much	chill
7	notch	ditch	match	fetch	catch		latch

53. **Blends** Clues

A game for small groups but could be adapted for class activity.

If children are having difficulty with 'r' blends, six of each blend 'tr', 'br', 'gr', and 'fr' words can be written on card. This makes 24 words and these words can be written on a chart or blackboard for display during the game. The backs of the cards have a clue in the form of a drawing or a colour: 'tr' blends – a tree; 'fr blends – a frog; 'br' blends – a brown shading and 'gr' blends – a green shading.

The pack is laid face down on a table and players take turns to draw a card and guess what the word is. The clue on the back of the card helps and the child may be saying 'tr' . . tr . . tr . .' before guessing the word. If the guess is correct s/he keeps the word, if not it goes to the bottom of the pack.

Children soon learn to listen for words that have 'gone' and concentrate on the words on the chart. Lots of practice in the particular blend is provided.

This activity can be adapted further without much explanation. We have used – for 's' blends:

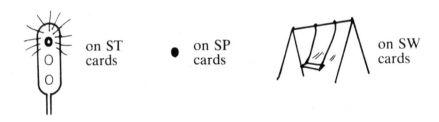

on ST cards   on SP cards   on SW cards

54. **Phonic Discrimination** Happy Families

A group game

Material: A pack of cards containing 'families' of four words, which may either be four words having the same digraph, e.g. 'read', 'seat', 'mean', 'team'; or words which have some irregularity in common. The number of cards to be used should be four times the number of players, with about eight extra.

To play: give each child four cards and put the rest of the pack face downward on the table; turn up the top card and lay it face upward beside the pack.

The aim of the game is to collect four cards in the same family. In turn, each child either takes the card showing, or one from the pack; s/he retains it, discards it, or discards another from his/her hand. As a card is picked up or discarded, it must be read. This continues until a child calls: 'Happy family'. S/he must then read the four words correctly. This game can be extended in size of 'family' and adapted according to need. It is a very popular game.

Variation: Collecting Happy Families

Where facilities allow, and with small groups, this method has been found specially successful with high-spirited children, and with older boys.

To play: scatter all the cards face down on tables or round the room. Players collect four of the *first* card picked up, replacing those not required. They should check what others are collecting, and be willing to 'give in' to another; otherwise, if several are looking for the same 'family' there will be a stalemate.

HAPPY FAMILIES
(by courtesy of Miss Q. R. A. Daniels)

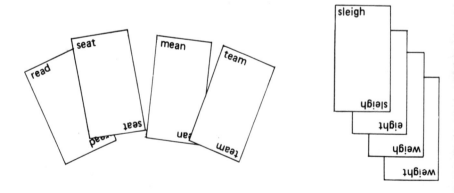

55. **Phonic Rule: Final 'e'**   Witch and Wizard

(by courtesy of Miss Q. R. A. Daniels)

To play: one child puts on the hat and is the witch if a girl, or the wizard if a boy.

The cards of three-letter words are scattered on the table.
The witch with the 'magic e' wand in her hand, asks a child to read a particular word. When this is done, she places the 'magic e' at the end of the word and says: 'With my 'magic e' I change 'a' into 'ay''. If the child reads it wrongly, s/he is handed a card with picture of a frog, snake, etc. on it, and, waving the wand over his or her head, the witch says. 'I turn you into a frog.'

With the next turn if he/she reads correctly, the child is changed back into a boy or girl.

The children take turns in playing the witch.

When the group is familiar with the change ă to ay the other vowels are taught one by one.

     i.e.   change ĭ into ī (as in kite)
               change ŏ into ō (as in rope)
               change ŭ into ū (as in tube)

WITCH AND WIZARD

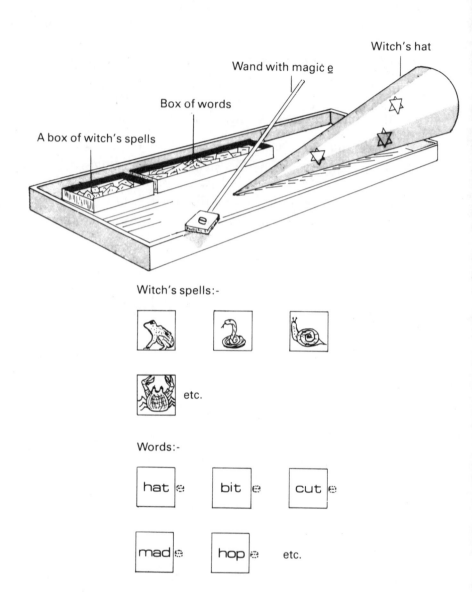

Witch's hat

Wand with magic e

Box of words

A box of witch's spells

Witch's spells:-

etc.

Words:-

hat e   bit e   cut e

mad e   hop e   etc.

READING FOR MEANING

To an extent, all reading is for meaning as readers attempt to make sense of the symbols, words, phrases and lengthier passages of text which face them daily. Wherever possible, the activity in classrooms should stress *meaning*. Children should understand the purpose of what they are doing and language should relate to children's perceived experiences. From children's earliest introduction to print, they should be encouraged to ask questions, interpret the pictures that accompany text, to comment upon the reading matter, make inference about the text and suggest alternatives. It is important that even when using word identification techniques the reader appreciates that what s/he is doing arises from the need to process meaning.

The following activities are designed to help children develop critical and insightful reading skills. They encourage analysis of the text, demanding that the child looks back or reads on, to express an opinion or make predictions. As the National Curriculum English Non-Statutory Guidance (1990) puts it, 'To become independent readers, children must learn to make choices from an early age'.

56. **Reading for Meaning**   Treasure Hunt

An active class game

Clues are written on pieces of card and placed in various hidden places in the classroom.

One child is then selected to be the first hunter and is given a card. S/he may read: 'The first card may be found behind the door'. This is read out aloud. If s/he fails on any word, another child is asked to read it and if successful s/he continues.
Having found the card it may say 'You will find the next card under my chair'.

The concepts *under, behind, in front of, through,* etc. can be stressed.

Many varieties of clue can be used:
'Look into the glass cupboard, you will see a green card';
'Walk to the piano, lift the lid – read the blue card there';
'The last card is in the paper basket'.

The whole class joins in the excitement of the 'hunt' and the hunter is rewarded with a star, team point or whatever.

When the game is played a number of times with different clues using a number of identical words, the weaker readers soon pick up these by activity.

57. **Reading for Meaning**   Number Codes

Some children, despite achieving a good mechanical reading age, seem to take an inordinate amount of time acquiring the facility of smoothness in reading. They may read words without understanding its meaning or its relevance to other words in the syntax. For these children this activity is recommended.

First step
The alphabet is written on blackboard and each letter is numbered 1 – 26, then familiar words are written in code on blackboard;

$$2, 1, 20 - bat$$

The children take fun in decoding and overlearning can take place if vocabulary from reader is employed.

Second step

To make children read for meaning, put messages in code which require a positive action on their part, e.g. 'Draw a bus', 'Take a sweet from my desk', 'You may eat your buns', 'Stand up', etc.

58. **Reading for Meaning**   Yes and No Game

Teacher writes a number of phrases, some true, some untrue, on card. Examples should be drawn as closely as possible from reading books in actual use by the pupils.

This is Peter . . .

Can a cat talk? . . .

A clock has a face . . .

Pupils work individually to insert Yes or No. When the task is completed the pupils pair up to read alternate lines and answers to each other.

59. **Reading for Meaning**   Synonyms

Pages of pupils' own written stories are reproduced for pairs of pupils to work on.

Teacher will have underlined certain chosen verbs and nouns and for each word underlined, provides a card upon which a similar meaning has been written. Pupils have to place the card on the underlined words. They then read the passage to see if the meaning has been maintained.

If this is too easy for some pupils they may be asked to supply their own synonyms. (Note: The National Curriculum orders for English require pupils to understand grammatical terminology. The use of games such as this one will enable pupils to appreciate that 'naming words' are nouns and 'doing words ' are verbs).

60. **Reading for Meaning**   Titles and Sub-Headings

Teacher prepares extracts from the beginnings of class reading books. Three alternative titles for each book and four alternative sub-headings at certain marked sections of the text are written down for the pupils so that they can decide on the most appropriate.

Title Example:-   *The Wind in the Willows*

Toad of Toad Hall

Tales of the River Bank

Mole's Adventures

Sub-Headings:-   *Happy Days*

Messing About on Boats

Surprise on the River

Mole Meets a New Friend

Pupils must give reasons for their response. They should also be encouraged to supply their own alternatives.

61. **Reading for Meaning** Sentence 'Halves'

Aim – To develop meaningful reading of sentences.

Materials: Using two different coloured cards, write out sentences from pupils' reading books – first part of the sentence on, say, blue card and its completion on, say, yellow card.

Method: Give no more than four sentences at a time, unless the reader is exceptionally able, otherwise the reader may find the exercise too difficult. Pupils can work independently or in pairs to match the sentence 'halves'.

Answers may be simply read or written and then read to teacher.

62. **Reading for Meaning** Cloze Sevenths

Aim – To develop meaningful reading via use of context.

Materials: A typed passage of roughly 70 words based on the pupils' reading level. Every seventh word should be deleted. The deleted word is written on small pieces of card which fit the size of the deleted words.

Method: Pupils work in pairs, attempting to solve the problem of the missing words before turning over the cards to check answers.

Scores out of ten should be recorded by pupils. This enables teacher to evaluate learning.

63. **Reading for Meaning** Choose Cloze

Aim – To develop insightful reading through personal choice of cloze procedure.

Materials: Reading books, strips of adhesive tape.

Method: Children, working in pairs, take turns to choose and cover with adhesive tape ten words from a suitable passage from the reader. Pupil who has covered the words then asks the second pupil to read the whole passage, including covered words. Adhesive tapes are removed and results recorded. Pupil roles are then reversed.

64. **Reading for Meaning** Detective Cloze-O

Aim – To develop critical reading skills.

Materials: Prepare typed passages from pupils' readers in which each line has a deliberately wrong word inserted.

Method: Pupils, working in pairs, underline the wrong word or simply note the number of the line, and write down the correct word.

When completed, pupils then check with the original text. This can be readily done if the text page number is marked at the top of the typed passage.

PAPER AND PENCIL GAMES TO IMPROVE READING
AND WRITING

Many of the games listed can be adapted to suit reading schemes or individual readers as appropriate, or to strengthen or reinforce particular reading strategies, e.g. phonics and other word attack skills. Whilst reading games can, by their very nature, provide opportunities for social training and personal growth through group interaction, it must be stressed that language and reading development must be planned, delivered through appropriate varied methodologies and monitored. Before these or any other reading games are played it is suggested that certain questions should be addressed:

- What is the purpose of this activity?
- What is the pupil expected to learn?
- What does the pupil expect to learn?
- How do we evaluate the activity and what has been learned?
- How did this fit the pupil's individual needs?
- What further educational objectives need to be planned?

Isolated games provide opportunities for only incidental learning and, whilst acknowledging that they may still have some value, it is generally agreed that pupils will make more progress if their needs are met through a planned and structured programme.

65. **Rhyming Snake**   (Reading and Rhyming Word Game)

Materials: Snake drawings (photocopied/duplicated by teacher or drawn by pupils.)
List of words *or* pupils' readers.

Method: Pupils work in pairs. Scan their list or book and write on the 'segments' of the snake the words that rhyme with the word written on the snake's tail by the teacher.

Example:

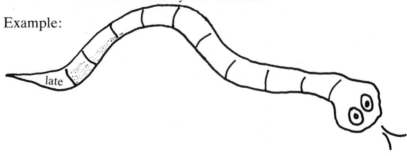

66. **Complete the Word Maze**   (Vocabulary Building)

Materials: Maze drawn on paper (see example.) List of words taken from children's readers.

Children work in pairs. They take turns in calling out any word from the list. When a word is called the other pupil writes it in the maze beginning at START. The child who gets to FINISH first wins.

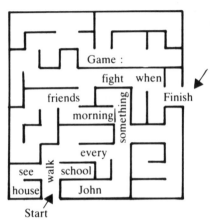

67. **Ladder Game**   (Use of Dictionaries)

Materials: Seven step ladders drawn on paper. Pencils. Dictionaries.

Method: Children write one letter on the bottom step, then a two letter word on the second step, and so on. Each word must begin with the same letter. When the ladders are completed the pupils read them to each other and they receive a point for each word where there is a mutual agreement as to its correctness.

Example:

garland	however
gather	hoping
great	house
game	home
get	him
go	he
g	h

68. **Ladder Race Game**   (Alphabetic Order)

Materials: Seven step ladders drawn on paper. Dictionaries.

Method: Start at bottom of ladder with a given letter. Pupils 'race' each other to write seven words which start with the same letter but where progressively alphabetic order applies to the *second* letter.

Example:

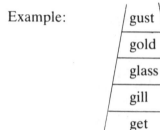

N.B.   For more adventurous games add more steps, or introduce a timing rule.

69. **Change a Letter**   (Vocabulary Building)

Materials: Paper and pencil.

Method: Start with a given word at top and work down to the line at the bottom.

Example:

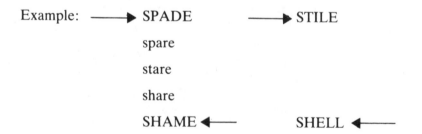

70. **Find a Word**   (Word Building)

Materials: Nine space square. Original word given.

Method: From the word given (in this case, 'aeroplane') make words where letters touch each other.

Example:

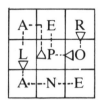

Rope; Peal; Lane; etc.

Pupils read their words to each other and receive a point for each one read.

71. **Story Line**   (Sequencing a story through sentences)

Materials: Sheet of lined paper. Pencils. List of words/phrases supplied by teacher. First line of story also supplied (as below).

Method: A number of players grouped around a table have a sheet of paper upon which the teacher has supplied the starting sentence. The paper is given to one of the group who reads the sentence and then writes a second sentence. (The person can write his/her own sentence entirely or choose to start the sentence from the list supplied.) After writing the second sentence, the second person folds the paper so that the first sentence is hidden. The paper is then passed to the third person who writes a third sentence and folds the paper so that the second sentence is hidden and passes the paper on.

The activity stops after an agreed number of turns. Stories are then read out and compared with other groups' products.

Example: Example of beginning sentence:

When walking through the woods I saw a strange man.

Examples of sentence 'starters':

After a while ....

Soon ....

Next day ....

Then ....

When s/he ....

It looked like ....

72. **Poetry – Group Composition**   (Language Discussion)

Materials: Selected short poems to suit the age group and levels of understanding. The poems are pasted on to card and then cut up into single cards.

Method: Pupils work in groups to form lines and stanzas of the poem. They are given the title of the poem and any support as thought appropriate by the teacher. Younger readers may need help, especially with the constructing of the first line.

When groups have finished they can compare product with other groups. Finally, teacher can read out the original. The object is not to see who comes close to the original but to develop creativity and stimulate discussion.

73. **Rhyming Lines**   (Develop Creativity and Phrase Construction)

Materials: Teacher provides paper with four line stanzas of which the second and fourth have been omitted. These can be published poems or lines created by the teacher.

Method: Pupils work together to supply missing lines and will need to discuss metre, rhyme, context and comprehension, style, and so forth.

Example: High above flies a silver plane

     ....

     Up and up in the deep, blue sky

     ....

Pupils read out the finished product and compare.

74. **The Slang Game** (Discussion of Standard and Non-Standard English)

Materials: Pupils are asked to note and record examples of slang that they pick up in everyday useage. Teacher lists on board or paper.

Method: Pupils discuss the list on display board or individual papers, working in pairs. On the left hand side is written the slang phrase/sentence and pupils have to supply the standard English equivalent.

Example: Gizzaciggyla? – I say, old chap, may I borrow a cigarette?

    Dyewannabutty? – Would you care to have something to eat?

USING GAMES TO DEVELOP THE SIGHT VOCABULARY OF A READING SCHEME

1. Starting with Book 1 of the scheme, write each word on an individual playing card. Make two packs. Put any number 1 – 6, on the back of each card. These cards can be used for playing Pairs (games 28) Grab (29) and Quickie (37).

2. On a sheet of A4 card draw a football pitch (hockey or rugby, to suit interests). The cards can be used to play the football game as described in 26.

3. On the reverse side of the A4 card make a Snakes and Ladder game using the above vocabulary. (See game 27 in this booklet).

4. Add the board from any commercial or home-made racetrack game *(Grand Prix, Grand National,* etc.). Racetrack games can be played using the cards, where progress around the track depends on correct reading and the number of spaces advanced corresponds with the number on the back of the card.
   (See game 33.)

   Note: The first book of most reading schemes today comprises about 16 - 24 words. Children developing smoothly might manage 16 new words in a game but for those experiencing difficulties eight new words or less will be sufficient.

5. The packs of cards and game boards with dice and counters should now be put into envelopes and suitably marked, e.g. Scheme: *Language Patterns,* Book 1.

6. This procedure should be repeated for Book 2 of the scheme. As this book will probably contain twice as many new words as Book 1, many more packs of cards and games will be required.

7. For Book 3 and beyond, the same procedure may be adopted although by Book 4 it may only be necessary to compile games from selected vocabulary which the teacher feels might provide some difficulty.

8. When the vocabulary of the whole scheme has been covered in this way children can be given the envelope relating to their level *prior* to going on to the appropriate pages in the book.

Suggested Use

Children should play the games with pupils at their level, although an adult or older good reader may need to referee. Teachers, however, should make a check on learned vocabulary before placing pupils on the appropriate page of the reading scheme.

A check on learned vocabulary could be made by inverting the pack of cards and asking pupil to turn one over and read the words aloud. If the pupil gets the word correct, s/he keeps it, if not, teacher keeps it. Further games and exercises can now be given using the cards held by teacher. Only when all the words are known should the pupil progress to the book. The teacher might first encourage pupils by pointing to newly-acquired vocabulary in the reader.

Fluency could be further stimulated by using the cards to indicate phrases to be read aloud.

By manipulating the cards and discussing phrases with the pupil both semantic and syntactic knowledge can be enhanced.

The provision of envelopes enables pupils to collect and return to a central store. If sufficient are prepared games envelopes can be taken home for some enjoyable homework, word check to be undertaken by teacher the following day.

Thus the teacher, once organised, is able to provide meaningful and appropriate learning experiences related to the class reading levels through which s/he can both control and assess progress.

Phonic work can also be structured by making games which illustrate all the phonic rules. (See games 42 to 55 in this booklet.) By classifying and having these put in labelled envelopes, children can be directed to the appropriate games whenever a particular phonic rule presents a difficulty.

USING GAMES TO DEVELOP PHONIC SKILLS

Flash Card Games

Many teachers make hundreds of flash cards; they put a great deal of time and work into the production of these cards but fail to derive from them the benefit that their work deserves.

Here are some suggested simple ways to derive maximum benefit.

1. Letter Cards.

   Aim – to teach initial sounds.

   Materials: 15 cards. Three each of e.g. a - b - s - t - m.

   Method: The 15 cards are placed on the table and the teacher says to each child alternatively - 'Pick up the card that starts **b**-ig or **b**-ed or **b**-at', emphasising the initial sound. If the child chooses the correct letter, s/he keeps it and of course, the child with most cards is the winner. The teacher gradually introduces new sounds until all the letter sounds have been learned.

2. Blend Cards.

   Aim - to teach initial blends.

   Materials: Start off again with about 15 cards, e.g. all the cards begin with the letter b. On the back of three cards write 'ba'; on three more 'be', then 'bi' then 'bo' and finally 'bu'. These are the combinations we want the child to learn. On the other side of the *ba* cards write e.g. 'bat' - 'bag' - 'bad'; on the *be* cards e.g. 'bell' - 'beg' - 'bet'; *bi* cards e.g. 'bin' - 'bit' - 'big'; *bo* cards e.g. 'box' - 'boss' - 'bog'; *bu* cards e.g. 'bus' - 'but' - 'bull'.

   Method: The cards are put down so that the children see only the two letters on the back. The teacher says 'Give me the card that says ba-ba-ba-bat. First of all, the child has to pick the right combination viz 'ba'. Should s/he get this correct, s/he may or may not get the correct word. It will not be necessary to work out this arrangement with all initial blends. Once the child has learned to work out a few blends, the rest often come fairly naturally.

3. As an extension to this game, the child should proceed to playing Pairs (see game 28) with the same cards. This time there must be two cards of each word; the teacher does not call out the words. All the cards are placed with the words downwards so the child can see only the first two letters of each word. S/he picks up a card with e.g. the letters 'be' on the back, and on turning it over finds the word 'beg' which s/he has to sound. Having done that, s/he must find another card which says 'beg'. The only clue s/he

has is that it starts with 'be'. So s/he must pick up a card with that combination on the back. Should s/he be lucky and pick up another 'beg', s/he keeps the pair of cards. Should s/he pick up a different word, s/he must place the two cards, face downwards on the table. This game not only helps the child to learn initial blends but also trains his/her memory, for, later in the game, s/he may pick up the other 'beg' and have to recall where s/he saw it previously.

4. The obvious stage after learning inital blends is to learn 'whole' words. The most suitable game here is probably Pairs (see 28). Ten words beginning with say, 'M', are chosen e.g. 'man' - 'mat' - 'mess' - 'mix' - 'mill' - 'mop' - 'mob' - 'mud' - 'mum'. Each word is written on two cards - a total of 20 cards and these 20 cards are used as in Pairs with the initial blends.

5. During this game of pairs, the child has been able to build the words, but will probably have seen and heard each word many times in the course of the game. We should now try to help the child recognise the word at a glance, in other words it should become a 'sight' word, and so we introduce the game of Grab (game 29). All the cards are scattered word uppermost, on the table. The teacher calls out a word and all the children look for it. The first to touch it takes the card. At the end the child with most cards is the winner.

This game may last only a minute or two, whereas it should last about ten minutes if it is to help all the children in the group. So we introduce a simple rule: should a child touch a wrong card, s/he must put back all the cards in his or her hand. As many of the words are very similar, it is easy for a teacher to catch the children out and so prolong a game for as long as seems necessary.

So far, we have outlined a flash card system of games devised to help children develop phonic skills. These games have been aimed at those children who have experienced great difficulty in the early stages of learning to read. The same games, of course, can be used for the child who is just starting reading. In this case, there may not be such a need for teaching phonics, but the same games can be played using the vocabulary of the reading scheme. If a child can be taught the words before being presented with a new book, s/he will find that the book will hold no terrors for him or her.

A simple reading kit can be contained in a large envelope, say A4 size, to hold a pack of flash cards, a Snakes and Ladders game, and a game of Bingo as described elsewhere in the book. If the three games deal with the same sounds or the same words, the children will have an enjoyable hour during which they will have played four games viz. Pairs (28) Grab (29) Snakes and Ladders (27) and Bingo. In the course of that hour, they will have seen and heard each word dozens of times.

An interesting exercise at the end of the period is for teacher to play Quickie (37). Teacher takes the pack of flash cards, slaps them down on the table one at a time, and leaves the card there for one second. The children endeavour to call out the word. The teacher will be agreeably surprised at the way in which the children quickly learn to recognise the words.

NOTES